Copyright © 2022

All Rights Reserved.

No part of this publication may be reproduced, distributed, or transmitted in any form or by any means. Including photocopying, recording, or other electronic or mechanical methods, without the prior written permission of the publisher, expect in the case of the brief quotations embodied in critical reviews and certain other non-commercial uses permitted by copyright law.

This Book Belongs To:

_ _

_ _

Alpaca

Bunny

Chick

I Spy with my little eye
Something beginning with ...

Duckling

I Spy with my little eye
Something beginning with ...

EIF

I Spy with my little eye
Something beginning with ...

F

Fairy

Gnome

I Spy with my little eye
Something beginning with ...

Hatch

I Spy with my little eye
Something beginning with ...

Iguana

I Spy with my little eye
Something beginning with ...

J

Jaguar

I Spy with my little eye
Something beginning with ...

Kangaroo

I Spy with my little eye
Something beginning with ...

Lent (Easter Lent)

Monkey

I Spy with my little eye Something beginning with ...

N

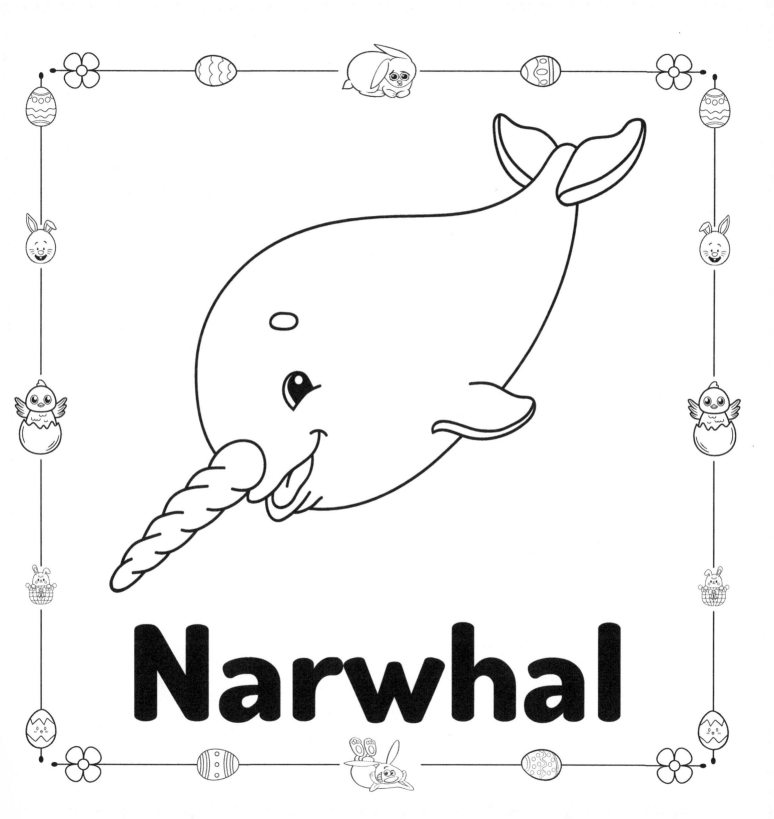

Narwhal

I Spy with my little eye
Something beginning with ...

Ox

I Spy with my little eye
Something beginning with ...

P

Pig

I Spy with my little eye
Something beginning with ...

Quail

I Spy with my little eye
Something beginning with ...

Rainbow

I Spy with my little eye
Something beginning with ...

Spring

I Spy with my little eye
Something beginning with ...

Tree

I Spy with my little eye Something beginning with ...

U

Umbrella

I Spy with my little eye
Something beginning with ...

Violin

I Spy with my little eye Something beginning with ...

Wolf

X-ray Fish

I Spy with my little eye
Something beginning with ...

Yak

I Spy with my little eye
Something beginning with ...

Zebu

Made in the USA
Middletown, DE
02 April 2023

28088218R00060